"十一五"期间国家重点图书出版规划项目

中国国家汉办重点规划教材

MONKEY KING CHINESE

美猴王汉语

（少儿）

编者：刘富华　王巍　周芮安

翻译：邵壮

北京语言大学出版社
BEIJING LANGUAGE AND CULTURE
UNIVERSITY PRESS

THE MONKEY KING

Sun Wukong, the Handsome Monkey King, is the hero of the Chinese literary classic *Journey to the West* (Wu Cheng'en, the Ming Dynasty). This novel was based on a true story of a famous Chinese monk, Xuan Zang (602 ~ 664). After years of trials and tribulations, he traveled on foot to what is today India, the birthplace of Buddhism, to seek for the Sutra, the Buddhist holy book. Finally he got the sutras and returned to China, or the Great Tang as was called at that time. He translated the sutras into Chinese, thus making contribution to the development of Buddhism in China.

In this novel, Buddha arranged for a monkey to become the monk's disciple and escort him, to ensure that he makes it to the west to get the sutras. The monkey called Sun Wukong, made the adventurous journey with Tangseng (the master), the other two disciples—Zhubajie (the pig-man) and Shaheshang (the monk) and Bailongma(the horse).

Sun Wukong was born out of a rock and fertilized by the grace of Heaven. In the Water Curtain Cave in the Mountain of Flower and Fruit, he was the King of the monkeys. Being extremely smart and capable, he learned all the magic tricks and kungfu from a Taoist master. He can transform himself into seventy-two different images such as a tree, a bird, a beast of prey or a bug as small as a mosquito so as to sneak into an enemy's belly to fight him or her inside out. Using clouds as a vehicle he can travel 108,000 *li* by a single somersault. The handsome Monkey King excelled in supernatural powers, defied hardships and dangers, and killed monsters. He protected his master Xuan Zang to overcome the eighty-one difficulties in fourteen years of the journey, and finally attained the Buddhist scriptures.

The Monkey King who is omnipotent, brave and winsome, is deeply beloved by Chinese children and adults alike even up till now.

To Teachers

Monkey King Chinese (school-age edition) is a series of elementary Chinese language primers for primary school children from the 1st year to the 3rd year in English-speaking countries. This series of textbooks is divided into three levels according to the year rank. Each level consists of two volumes, A and B. There are altogether six volumes and a total vocabulary of 251 words in the three levels.

Owing to a full understanding on the dispositions and learning habits of primary school pupils aged from six to ten in English-speaking countries, the editors have chosen topics which appeal to children and at the same time decrease difficulties of the contents to add more fun in the learning process. The aim of this series of textbooks is to give the children a preliminary understanding of the Chinese language through fun games and lay a good foundation for future systematic study.

The style and content arrangement of the textbooks are in accordance with the principle of progressing in an orderly and step-by-step way. Some topics among the three levels may be repeated but their difficulty is increased gradually. Words are the focus of the first level; phrases are the focus of the second level; and sentences the third level. The style and content arrangement of each level are as follows:

Level One: Words are the foundation, supplemented by Pinyin, nursery rhymes, handicrafts, and exercises, among which Pinyin are mainly single finals and tones.

Level Two: Word groups and phrases are the foundation, supplemented by Pinyin, nursery rhymes, handicrafts, and exercises, among which Pinyin are compound spellings of initials and finals.

Level Three: Short sentences are the foundation, supplemented by nursery rhymes, Chinese characters coloring tasks, words and expressions for everyday use, handicrafts, and exercises. Compared with the first two levels, Level Three has some simple Chinese characters, words and expressions for everyday use, and functions as a transition for regular Chinese language education.

Some suggestions to teachers:

1. Teacher leads the reading of words and expressions, sentences, nursery rhymes of each lesson using vocabulary cards, Pinyin cards, and CD.

2. Teacher can give some necessary explanations to the Chinese characters, handicrafts and the exercises. Then allow the children to freely express

themselves.

3. The task of teacher is to accompany children to learn Chinese through fun games. In the middle page of each volume there are "award stickers" and teacher can use them to award children as an encouragement.

4. It is not required for children to learn to write Chinese characters. They only need to learn to pronounce the Chinese characters by imitating and identify by coloring. It is enough for children to know that Chinese characters are square-shaped and have some objective senses of them.

5. The colored parts in each nursery rhyme can be substituted by other words and expressions in each lesson. Teacher can freely arrange class activities according to the nursery rhyme in order to make children practice words and expressions and sentence patterns repeatedly in the process of playing games.

We hope *Monkey King Chinese* will become a good friend of foreign primary school pupils just like the Handsome Monkey King—Sun Wukong.

Compilers

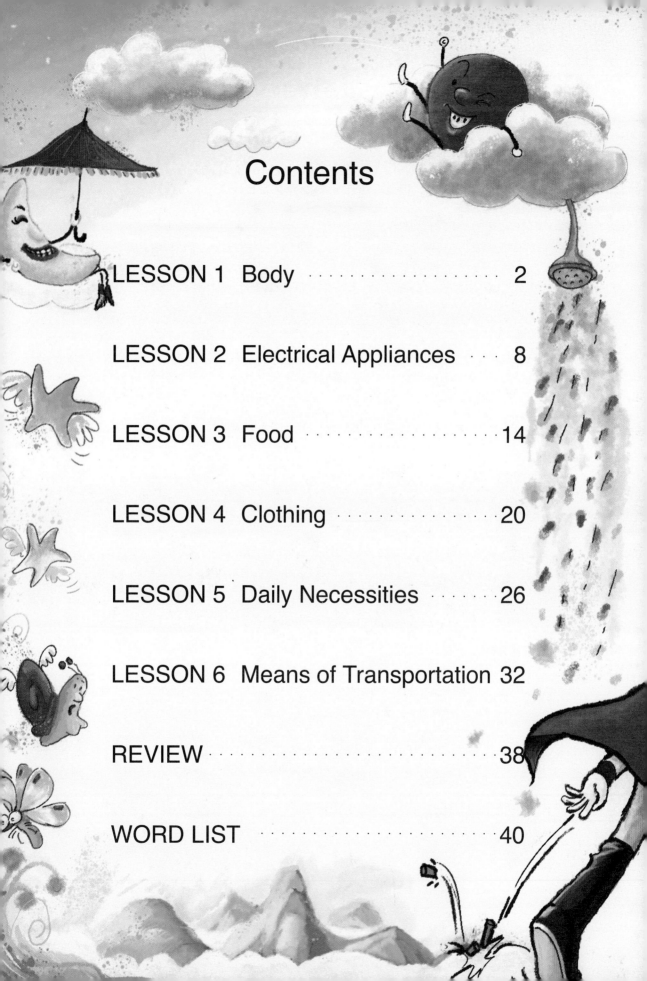

Contents

BODY

1. Say it.

tóu
头

yǎnjing
眼睛

ěrduo
耳朵

zuǐ
嘴

bízi
鼻子

shǒu
手

jiǎo
脚

2. Read it.

3. Chant it.

Mō mō yǎnjing,

Mō mō zuǐ.

Mō mō ěrduo,

Mō mō tuǐ.

Touching the eyes,
Touching the mouth.
Touching the ears,
Touching the legs.

4. Do it.
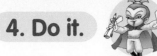

Color a dragon head.

Monkey King Chinese 1B

5. Exercises.

(1) Match.

ěrduo
耳朵

zuǐ
嘴

tóu
头

(2) Listen and draw.

(3) Read and stick.

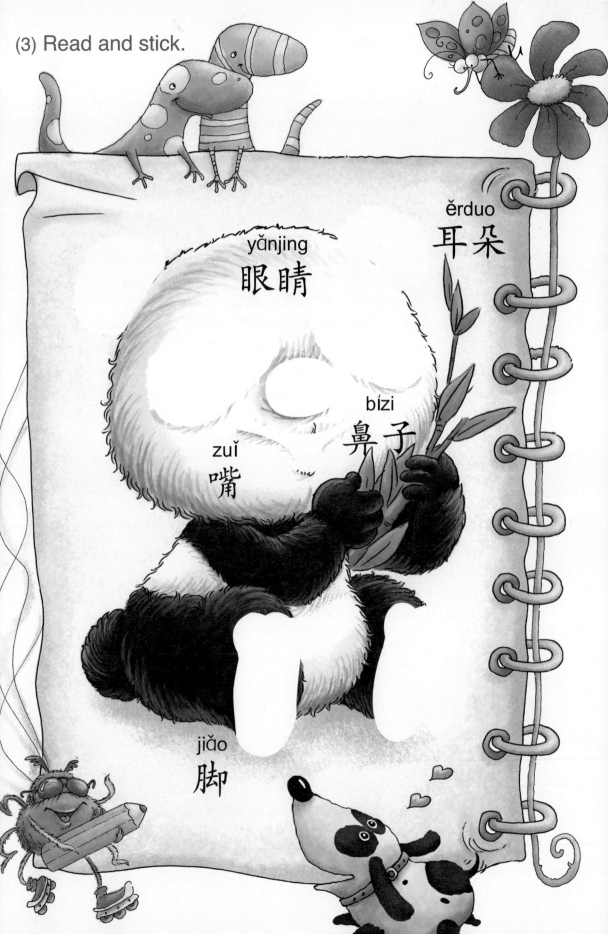

ěrduo
耳朵

yǎnjing
眼睛

bízi
鼻子

zuǐ
嘴

jiǎo
脚

ELECTRICAL APPLIANCES

1. Say it.

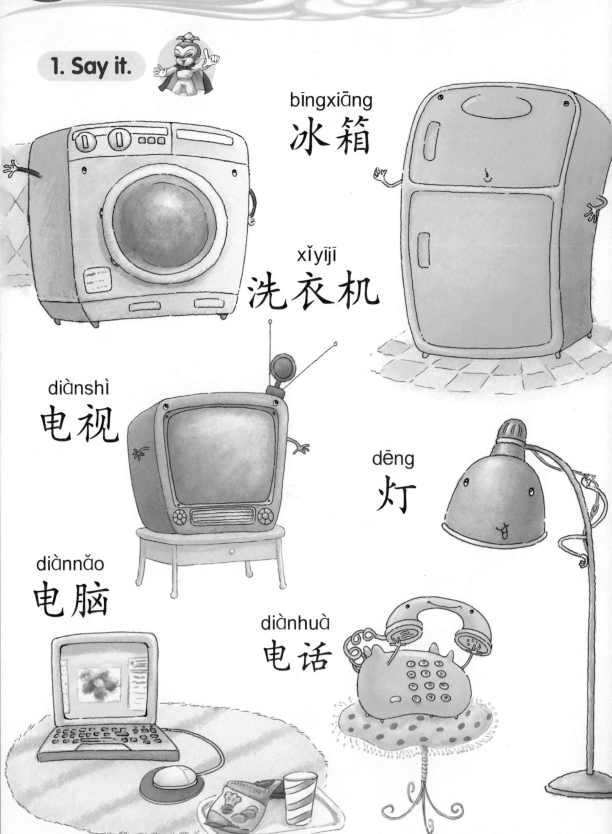

bīngxiāng
冰箱

xǐyījī
洗衣机

diànshì
电视

dēng
灯

diànnǎo
电脑

diànhuà
电话

2. Read it.

ong

ou

ong ou

3. Sing it.

4. Do it.

Fold a telephone.

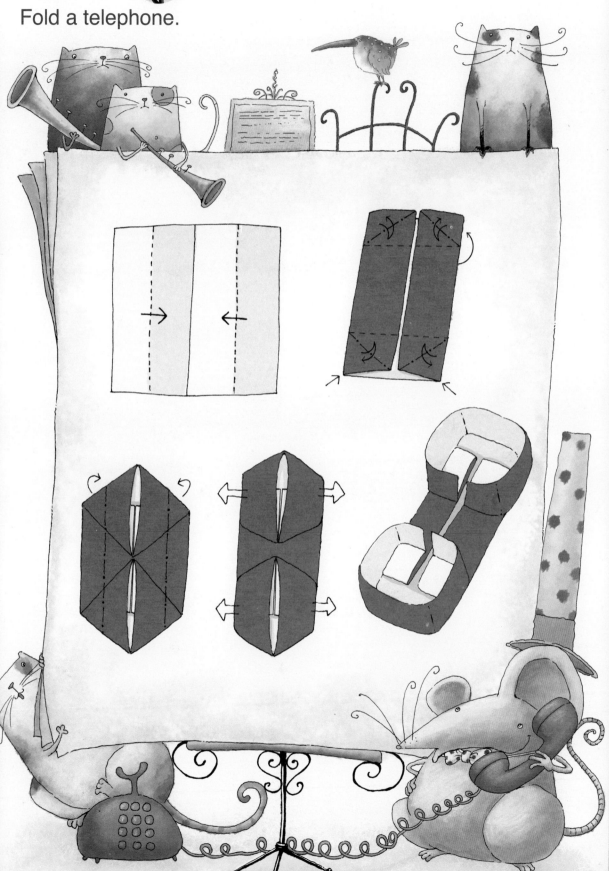

5. Exercises.

(1) Listen, choose and circle.

(2) Read and stick.

| dēng | diànnǎo | bīngxiāng | xǐyījī |

Monkey King Chinese 1B

(3) Find and match.

diànhuà
电话

bīngxiāng
冰箱

diànshì
电视

dēng
灯

FOOD

1. Say it.

jīròu
鸡肉

tāng
汤

hànbǎobāo
汉堡包

mǐfàn
米饭

miàntiáor
面条儿

niúpái
牛排

2. Read it.

e   ei   en   eng

Jīròu hé mǐfàn,

Hànbǎobāo hé tāng,

Zuò de zhēn hǎochī,

Yíxiàr dōu chīguāng.

Chicken and rice,

Hamburger and soup,

How delicious they are,

Let's eat them up.

4. Do it.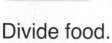

Divide food.

Please draw the favorite food onto each animal's tray.

5. Exercises.

(1) Listen and draw 😊 or 😞 .

①

②

③

④

(2) Find and match.

Alex

Michael

Wendy

mǐfàn   hànbǎobāo   miàntiáor

(3) Read and stick.

miàntiáor
面条儿

mǐfàn
米饭

niúnǎi
牛奶

tāng
汤

jīròu
鸡肉

CLOTHING

1. Say it.

kùzi
裤子

qúnzi
裙子

máoyī
毛衣

chènshān
衬衫

xié
鞋

wàzi
袜子

2. Read it.

ia ie iu ing

3. Sing it.

Zhī　Máoyī

织 毛衣

Moderato

作曲：汤韵

Zhè shì máo yī, zhè shì máo yī.

Máo yī zěn me yàng ?

Máo yī zhēn piào liang ,

máo yī zhēn piào liang .

This is a sweater.

This is a sweater.

What about the sweater?

It is very beautiful.

4. Do it.

Fold a small hat.

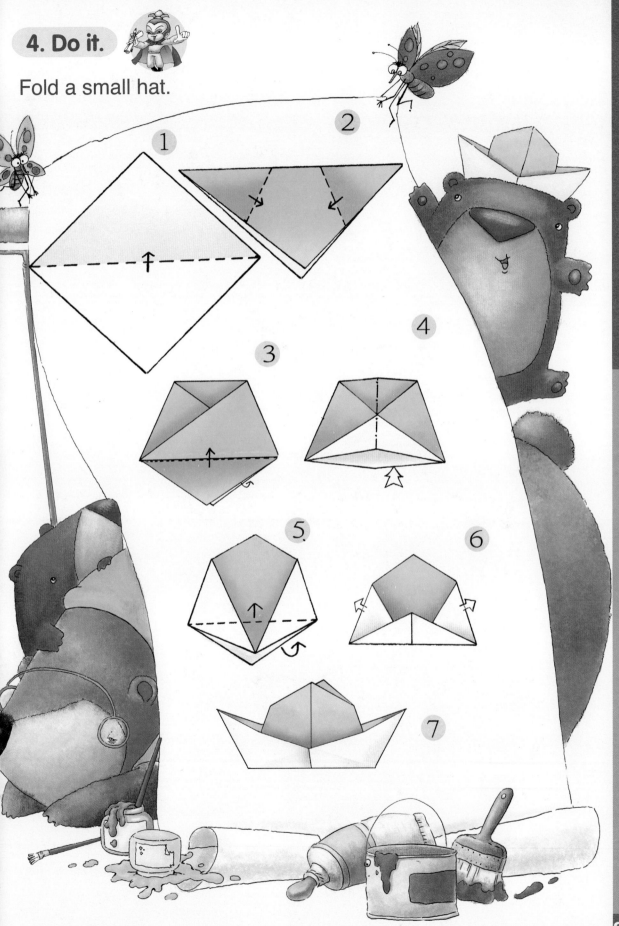

5. Exercises.

(1) Listen and color.

(2) Draw and join the dots.

chènshān

kùzi

xié

(3) Read and find the same ones.

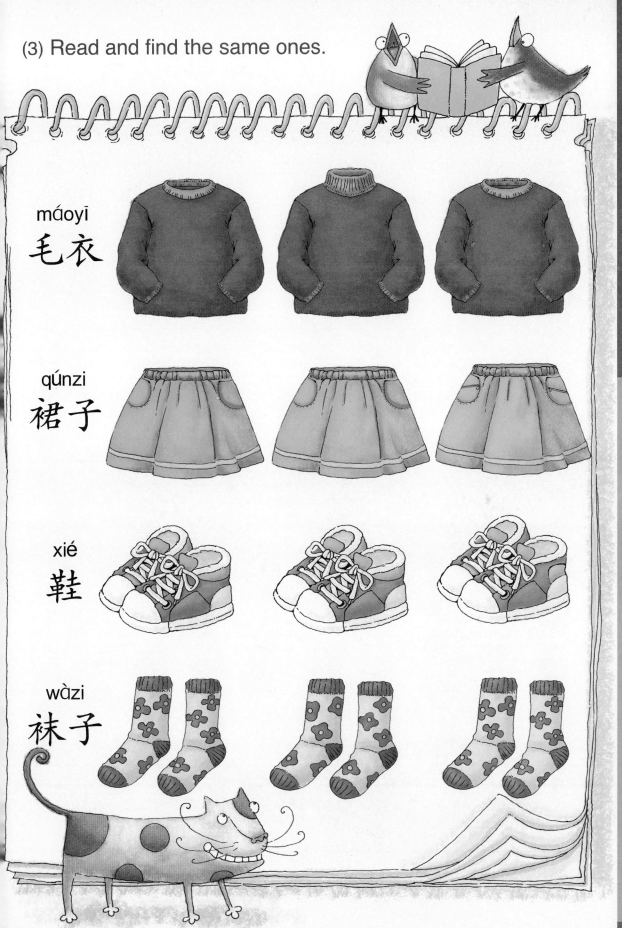

máoyī
毛衣

qúnzi
裙子

xié
鞋

wàzi
袜子

DAILY NECESSITIES

1. Say it.

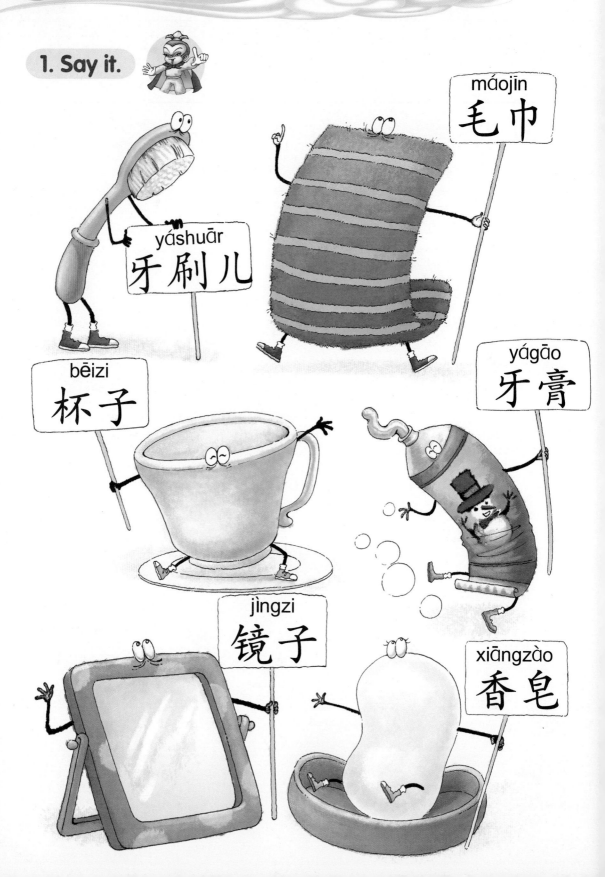

máojīn

毛巾

yáshuār

牙刷儿

yágāo

牙膏

bēizi

杯子

jìngzi

镜子

xiāngzào

香皂

2. Read it.

u

uo

ua

ui

un

3. Chant it.

Xiǎo xiāngzào,

Tiào ya tiào.

Xǐ ge zǎo,

Qǐ pàopao.

Small soap,

Is jumping, jumping.

Having a bath,

Sending up bubbles.

4. Do it.

Draw the missing parts in the picture.

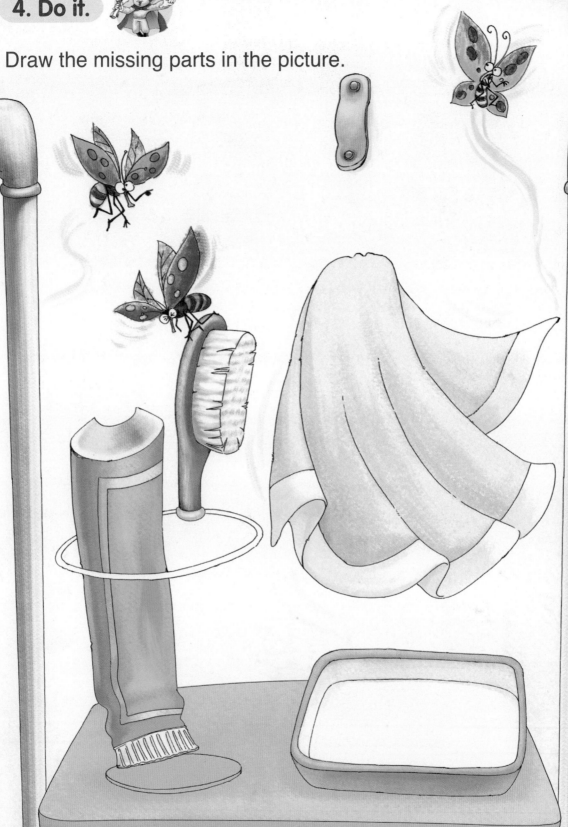

5. Exercises.

(1) Match.

máojīn
毛巾

jìngzi
镜子

yágāo
牙膏

xiāngzào
香皂

(2) Join the cups and guess.

What's this?

(3) Listen and circle.

Lesson 6

MEANS OF TRANSPORTATION

1. Say it.

qìchē
汽车

fēijī
飞机

lúnchuán
轮船

zìxíngchē
自行车

huǒchē
火车

mótuōchē
摩托车

2. Read it.

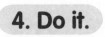 **4. Do it.**

Color, cut and stick a colored car.

Cut out the figures from supplementary page.

Monkey King Chinese 1B

5. Exercises.

(1) Choose vehicles for them.

lúnchuán	mótuōchē	fēijī	qìchē
轮船	摩托车	飞机	汽车

(2) Find the differences.

huǒchē

火车

(3) Read and color.

qìchē

汽车

zìxíngchē

自行车

毛衣

鼻子

脚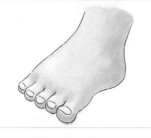

牙刷儿

汤

火车

裤子

耳朵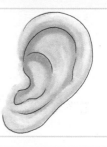

电话

衬衫

汽车

米饭

自行车

镜子

电脑

鞋

面条儿

杯子

电视

袜子

手

飞机

牙膏

眼睛

WORD LIST

B

杯子	bēizi	cup	5
鼻子	bízi	nose	1
冰箱	bīngxiāng	refrigerator	2

C

| 衬衫 | chènshān | shirt | 4 |

D

灯	dēng	lamp	2
电话	diànhuà	telephone	2
电脑	diànnǎo	computer	2
电视	diànshì	TV set	2

E

| 耳朵 | ěrduo | ear | 1 |

F

| 飞机 | fēijī | plane |

H

| 汉堡包 | hànbǎobāo | hamburger |
| 火车 | huǒchē | train |

J

鸡肉	jīròu	chicken
脚	jiǎo	foot
镜子	jìngzi	mirror

K

| 裤子 | kùzi | trousers |

L

| 轮船 | lúnchuán | ship |

巾	máojīn	towel	5
衣	máoyī	sweater	4
饭	mǐfàn	rice	3
条儿	miàntiáor	noodle	3
托车	mótuōchē	motor-bike	6
排	niúpái	beef steak	3
车	qìchē	car	6
子	qúnzi	skirt	4
	shǒu	hand	1
	tāng	soup	3
	tóu	head	1

W

袜子	wàzi	sock	4

X

洗衣机	xǐyījī	washing machine	2
香皂	xiāngzào	perfumed soap	5
鞋	xié	shoe	4

Y

牙膏	yágāo	toothpaste	5
牙刷儿	yáshuār	toothbrush	5
眼睛	yǎnjing	eye	1

Z

自行车	zìxíngchē	bicycle	6
嘴	zuǐ	mouth	1